UPWORK ESSENTIALS

*Start Getting Clients on Upwork
In 3 Days or Less*

John Morris

Idea Engine LLC

Copyright © 2023 Idea Engine LLC

All rights reserved. This book or any portion thereof may not be reproduced or used in any manner whatsoever without the express written permission of the publisher except for the use of brief quotations in a book review.

ISBN: 9798675411870
Printed in the United States of America
First Printing, 2020

Idea Engine LLC
PO Box 245
Winona, MO 65588

To the tens of thousands of freelancers who have taken my Upwork course over the years, this book wouldn't be possible without your support and feedback. Thank you! To my wife and kids... my reason for breathing.

CONTENTS

Title Page
Copyright
Dedication
Prologue
Day 1: Build an Upwork Profile That Ranks   1
Chapter 1: Rank and Relevance   2
Chapter 2: Pick a Niche   5
Chapter 3: Title and Categories   9
Chapter 4: Profile Picture   13
Chapter 5: Profile Overview   15
Chapter 6: Portfolio   20
Chapter 7: Specialized Profiles   24
Chapter 8: Projects   27
Day 2: Write Proposals That Get You Hired   31
Chapter 9: Upwork Is NOT a Numbers Game   33
Chapter 10: Start By Finding the Best Projects For You   35
Chapter 11: Find Projects That Fit   37
Chapter 12: Sift   40
Chapter 13: Qualify the Client   41
Chapter 14: Identify Key Hiring Criteria   43

Chapter 15: Write Your Proposal	47
Day 3: Juice the Algorithm	51
Chapter 16: BYOC	53
Chapter 17: Pick a Platform	56
Chapter 18: Build a Profile Pathway	58
Chapter 19: Fisherman Formula	60
Chapter 20: Get Social	62
Chapter 21: Promote	64
Chapter 22: TLDR	66
Appendix A: The Psychology of High-Paying Clients	68
Chapter 23: Turnkey	71
Chapter 24: Results-Oriented.	72
Chapter 25: Flawless	74
About The Author	75
Praise For Author	77

PROLOGUE

In my only mildly humble opinion, Upwork represents the greatest opportunity to start and build your own freelance business -- for the most amount of people across the largest range of countries, skillsets and circumstances.

Never before has there been such a large collection of eager buyers in one place that is as easily accessible to anyone willing to put forth the thought and effort to take advantage.

Those are also the reasons it's hyper-competitive.

This handbook is meant to be your guide to competitiveness. It certainly is NOT the end-all, be-all of freelancing of Upwork. For that, I recommend my full 6-hour Upwork course at: **https://myjohn.us/r2**.

This, instead, is a succinct guide to the essentials. A book you can read in just a few hours and have the "secret" to methodically building your Upwork business and outcompeting everyone else struggling to find the keys to the kingdom.

Sit down, take an hour and let me hand you those keys.

John Morris

DAY 1: BUILD AN UPWORK PROFILE THAT RANKS

Welcome to Day 1. In this section, we'll walk through building you an Upwork profile that BOTH ranks well in Upwork's search and suggestion engine AND is compelling to clients so they'll hire you.

Using the *Rank & Relevance Framework* I've refined again and again... both on my own and with the over 10,000 students I've helped build their Upwork businesses. Bottom line: this WORKS.

Then, in Days 2 and 3, I'm also going to show you how to write persuasive Upwork proposals and get traffic to your profile.

But, first things first...

Nothing matters if your profile isn't right.

CHAPTER 1: RANK AND RELEVANCE

Let's start with a bit of "theory". I put that in quotes because it's really not theory. It's been proven to me time and time again with student after student of mine.

When you build your profile, you need to recognize that Upwork's search and suggestion engine (the thing that decides if your profile is seen by potential clients) operates on two basic principles:

Rank and Relevance.

In basic terms, Rank is how good of a freelancer you are and Relevance is what projects you're the best fit for.

When a client submits a new project, Upwork analyzes it to figure out what categories it belongs to and what skills a freelancer would need to complete the project.

Then, Upwork looks through its freelancers to find the best ones with the skills needed for the project and it recommends those freelancers to the client.

A similar thing happens when a client searches for freelancers.

And the algorithm that handles all this is incredibly sophisticated. It's a lot like Google's search engine algorithm. Hundreds of "signals" help it figure all this out.

So to "win" on Upwork you need to do two simple things:

1. Do good work and get quality reviews
2. Send a clear signal to Upwork what you do

Rank and Relevance.

Now, here's the trick.

When you first start, *you have no Rank*. You haven't completed any projects ON Upwork. So no matter what you've done off-site, Upwork doesn't know you.

So, **it's going to test you**.

It will put you in front of some clients to see:

1. **Does your profile** convince clients to hire you?
2. IF a client hires you, are they happy with your work?

This is why your first few jobs on the site are critical. But, also, HOW you build your profile is critical. Does it "convert" -- to use marketing lingo. Remember, Upwork is a business not a charity.

If it puts your profile in front of some clients and they don't end up hiring you, it's essentially going to say "bad profile" and move on. It's got millions of other freelancers to analyze.

You need to help it.

And, the #1 way you do that is through Relevance. Relevance essentially breaks down to this:

1. Send a LOUD signal to Upwork **about exactly the kind of services you offer.**
2. Upwork suggests you to those and only those kinds of

projects.
3. Client sees you as a perfect fit for their project and hires you.
4. That project is added to your job history.
5. Upwork sees you as more relevant to *those* jobs.

And, the cycle builds on itself.

But, if you try to appeal to too many kinds of projects (at first), Upwork will suggest you to all kinds of projects, many of which will be a bad fit. Those clients won't hire you and Upwork will move on.

So, our job is to create that loud signal.

And, we do that with how we build your profile.

(Side note: This is, initially. As you work on projects, Upwork will rely more and more on your job history to determine Relevance. But, at first, you don't have that. So, it has to use your profile.)

With THAT context, then, we can build your profile the right way.

CHAPTER 2: PICK A NICHE

In the context of Upwork, a niche is a specific area of expertise or specialization that a freelancer focuses on. This can be a particular skill, industry, or type of work.

For example, you might specialize in web development for the healthcare industry, or copywriting for e-commerce businesses, and so on.

To really understand why picking a good niche is so important, let's do a little thought experiment.

Imagine you're the client and you're browsing through Upwork looking for a freelancer to hire. You come across two profiles that look almost identical. They have similar titles, overviews, portfolios, and skills. The only difference is that one has an extensive job history with lots of reviews, while the other has no job history and no reviews.

Now, ask yourself: which freelancer would you choose?

Chances are, you would go for the one with the job history and reviews. Why? Because as a client, you want to minimize your risk and ensure that you're hiring someone who can get the job done. Job history and reviews provide social proof and give you a sense of confidence that the freelancer has the skills and experience necessary to complete the project successfully.

So, what does this mean for you as a *new* freelancer on Upwork?

It means that you're at a disadvantage because you don't have a job history or reviews yet. You have to do something to get clients to pick you over the Upworkers with extensive job histories and tons of positive reviews.

So, what can you do?

Well, let's continue with the thought experiment.

Imagine you're the client again. And, imagine, you're looking for a WooCommerce developer and you come across two profiles. One has a generic title like "WordPress Developer" and mentions WooCommerce as just one of the many things they do. The overview talks about WordPress development, generally.

The portfolio is a mix of WordPress projects; some WooCommerce, some not. It has an extensive job history and lots of reviews, but it's not really targeted specifically to what you're after: a WooCommerce expert.

The other has a specific title like "WooCommerce Specialist" and talks only about WooCommerce in their overview. Their portfolio is only filled with WooCommerce projects.

Everything about the profile is oriented toward WooCommerce and WooCommerce only. No job history or reviews, but specifically targeted at exactly what you're after.

As a client, you're more likely to choose the second profile because they specialize in exactly what you need. They've demonstrated their expertise and experience in WooCommerce, which makes them stand out from the crowd.

Not every client will hire that 2nd profile. But, it gives you a fighting chance. It gives them a reason to at least consider you seriously. You stand out. You're different. And you speak to exactly what they need.

As a new freelancer on Upwork, it's your *only* chance.

If you don't have any job history or reviews, it's going to be tough to win clients over with your profile. But, if you specialize in a particular niche and orient your profile around it, you'll have a much better chance of standing out and getting noticed.

In addition, Upwork's algorithm is designed to match clients with freelancers who are the best fit for their needs. If you have a generic profile that mentions a little bit of everything, you're not going to show up as high in the search results for any particular job.

But if you specialize in a specific niche, like WooCommerce, Upwork will recognize that and show your profile to clients who are specifically looking for that type of freelancer.

That's why picking a good niche is so important. It not only helps you with clients, it also helps you with Upwork's algorithm. That's why so many of my students go from zero results on Upwork to suddenly getting tons of job invites after making the changes I recommend.

And, it all starts with picking a good niche.

So, what does a good niche look like? Here are some things to consider when picking a niche on Upwork:

It should be something you're passionate about and interested in. If you don't enjoy the work you're doing, you're not going to be motivated to do your best and you won't be happy in the long run.

It should be a marketable skill. There should be demand for the work you're doing and clients should be willing to pay for it. Upwork is perfect for this because you can type in any keyword to its search and see exactly how many posted jobs there are, how long ago they were posted, how much clients are paying and so on. The data is all there.

It should be specific enough to set you apart, but not so specific that there's no demand for it. For example, "WordPress developer" is a good niche, but "WordPress theme developer for eco-friendly dog grooming websites" might be too specific.

So, how do you go about picking a niche on Upwork? Here are some tips:

Look at your existing skills and experience. What are you already good at? What have you done in the past that you could potentially offer as a service?

Research the market. Look at what other freelancers are offering and what clients are looking for. Are there any gaps in the market that you could fill? Are there keywords with lots of projects coming through but low bid numbers or a low number of freelancers offering that service? Etc.

Consider your ideal client. Who do you want to work with? What kind of work do you enjoy doing? What industries or niches interest you?

Test the waters. Try offering your services in a few different areas and see which ones get the most interest. You can always adjust your niche later on if you need to.

Ultimately, a good niche is they key to this strategy and it's what so many new Upworkers don't do or don't spend much time on. They just pick "WordPress developer" or "graphic designer" or "writer" and don't give it much more thought, not realizing the consequences of that one decision.

To give yourself an easy advantage, take some time to think about your niche. Do a little research. Think about strategy. Don't overthink it, but don't brush it off, either. It's the major difference between those who succeed on Upwork and those who don't.

CHAPTER 3: TITLE AND CATEGORIES

Your Title is your clarion call to both Upwork and potential clients exactly what you do. It needs to be crystal clear. The standard approach is to create a "chain" of related keywords.

So, if you're a WooCommerce expert, your title might be:

"WooCommerce | WordPress eCommerce | WordPress".

You've likely seen this from other freelancers on Upwork. It's perfectly fine. In fact, this is what you'll want to eventually "evolve" to. But, in following our strategy, I recommend being ultra specific.

I prefer the "specialist" approach, like this:

"WooCommerce Specialist".

"Logo Design Specialist".

"Beauty Tips Content Specialist".

It makes it incredibly clear that you specialize in this one thing and this one thing only. In terms of sending a LOUD signal, this is screaming. The word "specialist" also has a certain feel to it.

That's why I prefer it to "expert".

Here are some additional tips for writing a title on Upwork:

Be specific: Make sure your title is specific and clearly conveys the type of services you offer. For example, instead of just writing "Developer," write "Web Developer" or "WordPress Developer."

Use relevant keywords: Include relevant keywords in your title that clients might search for. This will help your profile appear in search results when clients are looking for specific skills.

Be concise: Keep your title short and to the point. Upwork limits the number of characters you can use, so make sure your title is brief but informative.

Highlight your unique selling proposition: Think about what sets you apart from other freelancers offering similar services and highlight that in your title. For example, if you specialize in creating mobile-friendly websites, you could write "Mobile-Friendly Web Designer" as your title. (Side note: Simply being a specialist in exactly what the client needs is a kind of unique selling proposition).

Avoid using vague or generic titles: Generic titles like "Expert" or "Guru" are overused on Upwork and don't really say much about the services you offer. Try to be more specific and descriptive.

Test your title: If you're not getting the results you want with your current title, try experimenting with different titles to see what works best. You can always change your title later if you find something that works better for you.

Remember, your title is one of the first things clients will see when they come across your profile, so it's important to make a good impression and clearly convey what you have to offer.

Next, is your categories.

Here's where you get to tell Upwork, explicitly, what kinds of projects you want to work on. The big mistake here is listing anything and everything. That dilutes the signal.

It will put you in front clients with projects that don't fit.

Keep it tight.

Sticking with our WooCommerce example, I personally would only select the "Ecommerce Development" and "Web Development" categories. "Web and Mobile Design" is a potential fit, but I'm not a designer, so that's a bad fit for ME.

So, just look through the Categories and pick the best fits.

Less is more.

Here are some additional tips for selecting profile categories on Upwork:

Choose categories that reflect your skills: When selecting profile categories, choose the ones that reflect your skills and expertise. This will help clients find you when they search for freelancers with your specific skills.

Be specific: Upwork offers a wide range of categories and subcategories, so be specific when selecting the ones that apply to you. This will help you stand out from the competition and make it easier for clients to find you.

Think about your target market: Consider the types of clients you want to work with and the services you want to offer. This can help you determine which categories to select.

Check out the competition: Look at the profiles of other freelancers in your field to see which categories they have selected. This can give you an idea of which categories are most relevant for your skills and services.

Be open to change: As you gain experience and expand your skillset, you may want to add or remove categories from your profile. Keep an eye on the categories that are most relevant to your work and adjust your profile accordingly.

Overall, selecting the right profile categories on Upwork is important for making sure clients can find you and understand the services you offer. By being specific, considering your target market, and keeping an eye on the competition, you can create a profile that stands out and attracts the right clients.

(Side note: Upwork also lets you pick "Skills" to attach to your profile. Rules there are the same as Categories. Keep it tight. Less is more. Relevance over volume, etc.)

CHAPTER 4: PROFILE PICTURE

I'll keep this simple, but your profile picture needs to convey credibility not "cool" or "edgy". Remember, most of your clients will be business people. They're "squares"... like me :D.

Here are some tips for your profile picture on Upwork:

Use a professional photo: Avoid using selfies or casual pictures with friends. Choose a professional-looking photo that represents you as a freelancer. It's important to show yourself as someone who takes their work seriously.

Smile and look approachable: A smile goes a long way in making you look approachable and friendly. Clients want to work with someone who they can communicate easily with, so a friendly-looking photo can help.

Dress appropriately: Dress professionally in your photo, just as you would for a job interview. Avoid wearing anything too casual or anything with a lot of patterns or bright colors. You want the focus to be on you, not your clothes.

Keep it recent: Use a recent photo that represents what you look like now. You don't want clients to be surprised when they meet you in person or on a video call.

Show your personality: While it's important to look professional, you can still show your personality in your photo. Choose a photo that reflects who you are as a person and as a freelancer.

Use good lighting: Make sure the lighting in your photo is good and that your face is well-lit. Avoid using photos that are too dark or have harsh shadows.

Use a clear, high-resolution photo: Make sure your photo is clear and high-resolution. Avoid using blurry or pixelated photos.

Consistency across platforms: If you use your profile picture on other platforms such as LinkedIn or your personal website, make sure it's the same picture. This helps build your personal brand and makes it easier for clients to recognize you.

Remember, your profile picture is the first thing clients will see when they come across your profile on Upwork. A professional, approachable photo can help you make a good first impression and set you apart from other freelancers.

CHAPTER 5: PROFILE OVERVIEW

Now, we get to the big daddy. If your profile is how Upwork is going to determine which clients to suggest you to, your overview is the main way it's going to figure that out.

It's also how clients will decide to hire you or not.

So, it has to do double duty.

This is the nuts and bolts of the Rank and Relevance Framework. It's a 4-part framework that both sends that LOUD signal to Upwork AND is highly persuasive so clients will want to hire you.

So, let's dig in.

Part 1: Slipper Statement™

Remember Cinderella? She lost her slipper as she left the prince's ball and he searched his entire kingdom looking for the woman whose foot fit the slipper perfectly.

That's very similar to what your clients are doing. Searching the internet, Upwork specifically, for the perfect "fit". You need to give them a "slipper" to help find you.

THAT is the opening line of profile overview.

Here's an example:

"I specialize in building lightning fast WooCommerce websites for WordPress e-commerce website owners."

Breaking this down, there's four elements:

1. I specialize in... Just say this verbatim
2. Category: WooCommerce
3. Benefit: Lightning fast
4. Audience: E-commerce website owners

What you do, who you do it for and the ultimate benefit you offer. Your profile needs to start with this to make it crystal clear to potential clients (and Upwork) what exactly it is you do.

Remember, this might be the only thing a client reads before they decide if they want to look at your further. The closer a match you are to what they're after, the more likely they are to read further.

Clarity over clever.

Part 2: Proof

Now, you have their attention. Next, thing you have to deal with is their natural skepticism. Clients are jaded for the most part. At the very least, if they're going to part with their hard-earned dineros, they want to make sure they're not gonna get screwed.

So, we have to crank up the believability.

The big mistake here is trying to tell them what you WILL do. Every claim (about how great you are) that you make, imagine them responding with, "Yeah right. Prove it!"

Instead, you need to tell them what you HAVE done.

"I've built 63 WooCommerce websites for clients."

"I built a WooCommerce site for a client that does 1 million+ revenue."

"I increased the speed of a client's WooCommerce site by 63%."

Anything that seems relevant that you've done for other clients, you want to put here. Certifications. Awards. ANYTHING to prove you know what you're doing.

This can be hard if you're first starting out and you've haven't had any clients, yet. If that's you, I recommend doing some free projects for friends or family. Or, trying to find a certification if you can.

Do work just to put in your portfolio.

So, for nobody.

Those are still "sites built" or "logos designed", etc. We'll cover this more in the portfolio section, but you can include things that weren't necessarily for a client.

Again, ANYTHING you can put here to PROVE it.

Get creative.

Part 3: Process

If you've made it this far, the client is intrigued. They feel like they want to hire you, but they still have some fear of the unknown. You need to reassure them by getting rid of the unknown.

Best way to do that is to describe your process.

Here's an example:

> "When you decide to hire me, here's how we'll work together. First, click the hire button and complete the process on Upwork. Once hired, I'll schedule a call to discuss your project. I'll

> *determine milestones and provide you project roadmap. I'll complete your project according to the timeline. We'll have weekly phone calls to discuss any issues. Once complete, you'll sign off that the project is complete. At that time, payment will be due. I ask that you leave a review, good or bad, so I know how I did"*

Something like that. You don't have to do phone calls or include the stuff I did. But, you need to describe "what will happen" once they do hire you. So, the unknown becomes the known.

This gets them over the hump to hiring you.

Which leads, finally, to:

Part 4. Call-To-Action

Ask for the sale to use sales lingo. This can be really simple, but it needs to be there. So, for example:

"If you're ready to get started, simply click the 'Hire' button and I look forward to talking with you."

Nothing crazy.

That said, your call-to-action is what sales and marketing pros call a "close". And there are several different types of closes you can use:

Soft Close: This is a non-aggressive approach that involves gently nudging the client towards hiring you. For example, you might say something like "I'm really excited about this project and I'd love to be a part of it. Let me know if you have any questions or if there's anything else I can do to help." This approach is generally best for clients who are on the fence or who need a little bit of reassurance before making a decision. Or, simply asking them to send you a message to chat about their project instead of asking them to just immediately hire you.

Hard Close: This is a more direct approach that involves pushing the client to make a decision. For example, you might say something like "I'm confident that I'm the right person for this job, and I'm ready to start working right away. Can we get started today?" This approach is generally best for clients who are actively looking to hire someone and who are just waiting for the right person to come along. My earlier example from this section is an example of a hard close.

Time-Limited Close: This is a variation on the hard close that involves creating a sense of urgency by setting a deadline. For example, you might say something like "I'm really excited about this project, but I have a few other offers on the table. If we don't move forward in the next day or two, I might have to take another job." This approach can be very effective for getting clients to make a decision quickly. Not likely to be used on your profile, but could be useful when messaging with a potential client.

Assumptive Close: This is an approach that involves assuming that the client is going to hire you and acting accordingly. For example, you might say something like "I'm really looking forward to getting started on this project. Can you send me the details so I can get started right away?" This approach is generally best for clients who are already leaning towards hiring you, but who just need a little bit of a nudge to seal the deal. This is my favorite close. Most people hate making decisions and this close takes that pressure off of them because you're essentially make the decision for them.

And, that's it. Whew! It's a lot, but you only have to do it once. And, if you put in the time and effort here, it's going to pay dividends for you. Most people simply don't do this.

And, that's why they struggle on Upwork.

CHAPTER 6: PORTFOLIO

Your portfolio is often the first thing a client will look at, especially if you're in a visual niche like graphic design or web design. It will do the bulk of the "selling" for you.

So, it needs to be on point.

A couple rules here:

- Less Is More
- 1 > 0
- Seeing Is Believing

Let's talk about each one:

Rule #1. Less Is More

Most people's impulse is to stuff as much of their past work into their portfolio as possible. That's a mistake. Why? Because, no client is going to go through your whole portfolio.

They're going to click through on items that interest them.

What happens if the one they click isn't 100% your best work? It happens to everyone. Some of our work is better than others. We want to ensure clients see our best work.

So, only include your absolute best projects in your portfolio. That way, no matter what they click on, they get the best stuff.

Rule #2. 1 > 0

This is a famous Gary Vanyerchuk line and it absolutely applies to your portfolio. Something is better than nothing. An empty portfolio is the worst thing you can "show" to a client.

Now, if you're new and don't have any client work, that's fine.

GET some work.

Do it for free. Just create something on our own solely for the purpose of putting in your portfolio. Whatever you have to do, you NEED something your portfolio.

Nothing will turn a client off faster.

Rule #3. Seeing Is Believing

Visual appeal. Like it or not, it's a thing. How many times have you decided NOT to install an app on your phone because the icon or interface was ugly? I do it all the time.

No matter what you do, add visual appeal to your portfolio.

I know it can be hard for certain niches, but do your best. The more visual appeal your portfolio (and projects, for that matter) has, the more likely a client is to look through it and be impressed.

And, again, your portfolio is the main way a client gets "sold".

So, this is critical.

That said, here are some additional tips for creating a winning portfolio on Upwork:

Showcase your best work: Yes, we covered this, but it bears repeating. Your portfolio is essentially your showcase, so make sure you're highlighting the best work you've done. Choose projects that demonstrate your skills and expertise, and make sure the work is presented in a clear and organized manner.

Keep it relevant: Your portfolio should be relevant to the type of work you're looking to do on Upwork. If you're a graphic designer, for example, make sure you're showcasing your design work rather than unrelated projects.

Use high-quality images: If your portfolio includes images, make sure they're high-quality and showcase your work in the best possible light. Poor quality images can detract from the overall impression you're trying to make.

Provide context: Make sure you're providing enough context for each project you showcase. What was the client's goal? What challenges did you face? How did you approach the project? Providing this kind of detail can help potential clients better understand your work and your approach.

Be concise: While you want to provide enough detail to give potential clients a good understanding of your work, you also want to be concise. Keep your portfolio brief and to-the-point, highlighting the most important details.

Keep it up-to-date: Finally, make sure you're regularly updating your portfolio with new projects and removing outdated work. This shows that you're actively engaged on Upwork and keeps your portfolio fresh and relevant.

Ultimately, your portfolio on Upwork is one of the most important aspects of your profile. It's your chance to showcase your skills and expertise to potential clients. It's a visual representation of what you're capable of and what you've accomplished. When done well, a portfolio can set you apart from the competition and convince clients to hire you.

Remember, clients want to see what you can do and how you can help them. Your portfolio is your chance to show them that you're the right person for the job. So take the time to create a strong portfolio, and make sure it's always up-to-date with your latest work. By doing so, you'll increase your chances of landing your next project on Upwork.

CHAPTER 7: SPECIALIZED PROFILES

Specialized profiles are a way to create additional profiles on Upwork that showcase your skills and experience in specific sub-niches of your field. This allows you to tailor your profile to a particular area of expertise and demonstrate to clients that you have the skills they're looking for.

Think of your main profile as your general resume, while specialized profiles are like targeted resumes. You can create a specialized profile for each sub-niche that you want to target, whether it's "wordpress theme developer" or "translation for legal documents." Each specialized profile can showcase your specific skills and experience in that area, making it easier for clients to find the right freelancer for their job.

But the best part? You can use specialized profiles in addition to your main profile - so you're not limited to targeting just one area. This means you can cast a wider net with your main profile while still highlighting your expertise in specific sub-niches with your specialized profiles.

In this chapter, I will show you how to use your specialized profiles in a strategic way to methodically build your Upwork profile to dominate large, high-traffic keywords.

Let's get started.

Main Profile

Ultimately, you want to rank for large, high-traffic keywords on Upwork. Something like "wordpress developer" or "graphic designer". If you consistently rank for these kinds of keywords, you'll have more work than you know what to do with. In addition, when you rank high for these large keywords, you'll tend to dominate all the smaller, long-tail keywords associated with them.

So, this is the long-term goal and you should build your main profile around whatever keyword that is for you.

However, those keywords are also extremely competitive. Everybody wants to rank high for them. So, trying to rank for them when you're brand new is almost impossible. Thus, our strategy here.

Specialized Profiles

Once you have your main profile set up and optimized for your high traffic keyword, it's time to start creating specialized profiles to target sub-niches within your area of expertise.

The idea here is to create specialized profiles that target specific keywords related to your main keyword. For example, if your main keyword is "WordPress developer," you could create specialized profiles targeting sub-niches such as "WordPress theme developer," "WordPress plugin developer," or "WordPress website speed optimization specialist."

These niches are off less competitive. By targeting them, you'll have a better chance of showing up in search results when clients are looking for these very specific skill sets. This can help you stand out from the competition and increase your chances of landing more jobs.

The big benefit of using specialized profiles is that they allow you to build up your job history that's still related to the main keyword you're targeting on your main profile. So, you're getting the best of both worlds. You're targeting smaller, less competitive keywords to get started, but still building a job history that will help you rank higher for your main keyword.

This is one of the things most Upworkers don't do that kills them. They just try to go right for a large, high-traffic and highly competitive keyword and end up getting nowhere.

Of course, it's also important to make sure you're specialized profiles are optimized for search. This means including relevant keywords in your profile headline, summary, and portfolio descriptions.

By creating specialized profiles and targeting sub-niches within your area of expertise, you'll be able to increase your visibility to potential clients and improve your chances of landing more jobs on Upwork -- and you'll be implementing a proven strategy to methodically build your Upwork profile to rank at the top of large, high-traffic keywords.

CHAPTER 8: PROJECTS

Upwork's Fixed Price Projects are pre-packaged services that freelancers can offer to clients for a fixed price. These services can be anything from designing a logo or creating a website to providing social media management or writing blog posts.

One of the benefits of offering Fixed Price Projects is that it can save time for both the freelancer and the client. Rather than going through the traditional proposal and bidding process, clients can purchase a project directly from the freelancer that meets their needs.

This can be particularly useful for clients who have a specific project in mind and don't want to go through the process of reviewing multiple proposals.

For freelancers, offering Fixed Price Projects can help them attract clients who are specifically looking for a particular service or skillset. Additionally, it can help them streamline their services and create a more efficient workflow.

By creating a clear description of the work they will provide and setting a fixed price, freelancers can eliminate the need for negotiations and potential miscommunications with clients.

To use Upwork Fixed Price Projects, freelancers first need to create a project description that clearly outlines the work they will provide. This should include a detailed scope of work, any necessary deliverables, and the timeframe for completing the project. Additionally, freelancers will need to set a fixed price for the project.

Once the project is created, it will be visible on the freelancer's Upwork profile and can be purchased by clients directly. It's important to note that freelancers are responsible for delivering the project within the agreed-upon timeframe and providing any necessary revisions to the client.

Best practices for using Upwork Fixed Price Projects include:

Pick relevant projects. Again, the ultimate goal is to build up a job history that helps you rank higher for the keyword your main profile is targeting. So, pick projects that are highly relevant to that keyword.

Clearly define the scope of work. Before creating a fixed-price project, make sure you have a clear understanding of what the project entails. Clearly define the scope of work so that both you and the client know exactly what is expected.

Keep the project title short and descriptive. Use keywords that describe what the project is about and make it easy for clients to understand what you're offering.

Write a clear and concise project description. Be specific about what the project entails, what the deliverables are, and what the client can expect to receive. This will help manage expectations and reduce misunderstandings.

Price the project appropriately. Research what other freelancers are charging for similar projects and price your project accordingly. Make sure your pricing is competitive but also reflects your experience and expertise.

Provide examples of your work. Showcasing your past work or providing sample deliverables can help potential clients understand the quality of your work and what they can expect from you.

Set clear milestones. Break the project down into clear, manageable milestones and set deadlines for each one. This will help you and the client stay on track and avoid delays.

Offer revisions. Providing revisions to your work can help build client satisfaction and trust. Make sure to clearly outline how many revisions are included in the project price.

Use clear and concise language. Use language that is easy to understand and avoid technical jargon or industry-specific terms that clients may not be familiar with.

Be responsive to client inquiries. Respond to client messages and questions in a timely manner to demonstrate your professionalism and build trust with potential clients.

❋ ❋ ❋

And, there you go. There are a few other parts to your profile but the parts I've covered here are the main ones in terms of sending that LOUD signal to Upwork.

Get these right and you're much more likely to start showing up for the right kinds of projects and getting clients to the point of wanting to hire you. Then, it's on you to do good work from there.

And, Upwork is your oyster.

In the next chapter, we're going to dig into bidding on projects and writing your proposals. Both, finding the highest-paying projects that are a good fit AND writing your proposals in a way that gets you hired.

Specifically, uncovering the K__ H_____ C_____ for each project.

When you know that, "what to say" in your proposal becomes simple and easy. It's like having the "cheat codes" to your client's "Yes" button. So, we'll dig into that tomorrow.

Now, as a side note....

If you're really committed to Upwork and serious about making it work for you. And, you want to dig further into all this and really nail the detail and nuance and get it perfect...

I have a full 6-hour video course where I walk you line-by-line through building your Upwork profile, writing proposals and getting traffic to your profile.

I not only show you what to do, but how to do it. How to come up with the right answers for "what's my niche" and "what should my overview say, exactly" and so on.

If you're interested, you can learn more about the course here: https://myjohn.us/r2

DAY 2: WRITE PROPOSALS THAT GET YOU HIRED

Yesterday was a doozy, eh? But, critical. We'll talk a little more about why, in this section, as well, but, I hope you had a chance to rework your profile before moving on.

Now, though, it's proposal time.

This is fun, because we get to move from waiting for clients to hire US to going out and getting them. When you get this down, it really does start to feel like you can write your own check a bit.

Couple THAT with what I'll teach you tomorrow and... **Well, let's not get ahead of ourselves.**

Second things second.

Let's talk proposals.

Just like with your profile, there's some context here that matters. You're not writing proposals in a vacuum. You can write the greatest proposal in the world, but if you're bidding on the wrong jobs?

JOHN MORRIS

It ain't gonna matter.

So...

Let's dig in.

CHAPTER 9: UPWORK IS NOT A NUMBERS GAME

By far, the biggest mistake I see, when it comes to proposals, is treating it like a numbers game. Finding a bunch of jobs loosely related to what you do, blasting out a copied and pasted proposal to all of them and waiting for the clients to roooooooll in!

Aaaaand... crickets.

Has this happened to you? Hopefully, with everything we talked about regarding Rank and Relevance in the last section, you now have some idea why. Upwork is all about "fit".

A tight fit between client and freelancer.

Randomly blasting out a bunch of copied and pasted proposals to loosely-related projects is NOT trying to create a good fit. It's the exact opposite, in fact.

So, don't do it.

Upwork has also tried to discourage that practice by charging for Connects. By and large it's actually worked pretty well. People

JOHN MORRIS

think a little harder about what jobs they bid on now.

CHAPTER 10: START BY FINDING THE BEST PROJECTS FOR YOU

Now, that we understand it's not a numbers game the question becomes: what DO we do? Again, it goes back to "fit". You need to actively find projects that are the best fit for you.

Not only are you more likely to get hired, you're more likely to deliver at a high level. Which gets you a high rating and quality review and the snowball starts rolling in your favor.

Upwork will begin "sending" you more of THOSE jobs.

You'll do a good job.

More ratings and reviews.

More of those jobs.

You get the picture. THIS is how we turn Upwork in our favor and suddenly you look back a few years later and you've made 200K on the site... or whatever it is.

Momentum.

JOHN MORRIS

So, HOW do we do it?

CHAPTER 11: FIND PROJECTS THAT FIT

You'll want to become a search expert. This one thing can make such a big difference. Remember the marketing axiom (which is really what we're doing here):

"The right message in front of the right people in the right medium."

Or, said another way you might have heard:

"Message to market match."

Well, we're already on the right medium... Upwork. It's a site filled with people ready to "buy". Doesn't get much better than that. Our "message" is our proposal.

BUT, we've got to put it in front of the right people.

Otherwise, it won't matter.

So, head over to the Upwork search and type in your primary search term. If you followed the instructions in the last chapter and picked your ONE single niche, this should be pretty obvious:

"woocommerce"

"wordpress speed optimization"

"logo design"

Whatever that is for you.

Then, click the "Filters" button in the top right.

First, change the Sort to "Relevance". You can bounce between "Newest" and "Relevance", but I like to start with the most relevant projects to my search query.

Next, you need to go through each filter and select ONE option that is the best fit for what you're looking for.

Do you want hourly or fixed?

What's your experience level (honestly)?

What budget do you prefer AND deserve?

On through all the filters until you've selected the criteria that are the absolute best fit for who you ARE and what you WANT. Don't worry about how many jobs there are.

You first need to understand fit.

Then, run the search.

This should narrow you down to 20 or less jobs. In some cases, less than 10. Depending on your niche, it could be none. But, that's okay. Now, you know.

But, this list is your PRIME list.

These should be the absolute best fit for you. They're the jobs you want to spend extra time reading, analyzing and writing a proposal for. As with everything Upwork, less is more.

Next, thing to do is save the search.

That way, you can quickly come back to this each week.

Now, here's where I lose a lot of people. Don't get discouraged if there's no jobs listed or very few or you bid on all these and don't get hired. Again, this is our strictest criteria.

What you do next is the *Ripple Method*^{TM}.

Go back into the filters and expand your criteria just a bit. So, maybe you prefer fixed priced projects, BUT you'd do an hourly project if you had to. Or, you prefer clients with 10+ hires, but you'd accept less.

Create a next "tier" of relevance.

Not exactly the most perfect fit, but close.

You'll notice each new filter you expand on will dramatically increase the number of jobs in the list. So, don't do a whole bunch at once. Remember, you can't even bid on 100 or 1,000 jobs.

So, expanding out that quickly isn't useful.

Look for the filters that increase the job count by just a little bit. That keeps you very close to your ideal project, but increases the number slightly to give you more "at-bats".

Play with it a bit.

And once you find a second set of filters you like, save those. Do this again for a third tier, expanding ever so slightly and then save that, as well. For most people, that's probably enough.

It depends on the niche, but for most, 3 tiers is usually enough.

You'll be looking at more jobs than you could ever bid on.

CHAPTER 12: SIFT

Next, you'll want to do a quick "sift" of the projects list. Look through each project and do a quick analysis of whether or not it's the kind of work you want to do.

We're not reading the project in detail or analyzing clients, yet.

Just a quick sift of the project itself.

Budget.

That kind of thing.

Any that you think are a good fit, click the "Save Job" button on. That'll add it to your "Saved Jobs" list which will become your primary list of jobs you're going to spend time analyzing and bidding on.

You're aiming for 15-20 jobs here.

Ripple out on your tiers from the step before if you have to. But, if you get to 15-20 on your first tier, don't bother. There's no reason to do that work if you don't have to.

Once your Saved Jobs list is populated, now we can...

CHAPTER 13: QUALIFY THE CLIENT

Each project contains a section, on the right sidebar, that says "About the Client". Give it a quick look. What kind of ratings have other freelancers given the client.

What's their hire rate?

How much have they spent on the site?

Here we're not looking for perfect, instead we're looking for terrible. We want to weed out clients who DO have a history on the site and it's awful. We do NOT want to work with them.

So, if a client has a 3-star rating, a 20% hire rate and has spent $20 over 10 projects... I don't care what they say their budget for THIS project is, I'm not gonna waste my time.

That said, I'd take the total spend with a grain of salt.

We don't know what projects that was for. Maybe they hired someone to walk their dog and paid them $10/hour. That might be a good rate for that project, but terrible for building a complicated website.

Hire rate and reviews, though.

They tend to tell the tale.

One other caveat...

Don't automatically disqualify new clients. Some won't have much of a history on the site because they're new. That doesn't mean they're bad. A new client could turn out to be a GREAT one.

So, I don't weed those out.

That's up to you, though.

So, go through your 15-20 and weed out the worst ones. Remove them from your Saved Jobs list. If doing that brings you down to say 2 projects, then go back to Step 1, circle out a tier (if you have to), sift and add some more projects.

What we're after is roughly 5-10 projects left after our client analysis.

That's about the most you're going to be able to realistically bid on in a week and produce a quality proposal. It does depend on your niche a bit, but that's a good rule of thumb.

Last step before we write our proposal, then, is to...

CHAPTER 14: IDENTIFY KEY HIRING CRITERIA

If you've done everything up to this point, you are set up for success. You're on the right medium. You're staring at a list of the right people. Now, we just have to craft the right message.

But, HOW do we do that?

We can't just sit down and write something generic. Every client is different. Different values, different beliefs, different wants and needs. The "right" message is the one that's perfect *for that client*.

To know what that is, you need to analyze their project.

And, figure out what their Key Hiring Criteria (KHC) are.

Every client has them. They're just different. Some value speed. Others, communication. Some are terrified of getting screwed. Once you find those hot buttons, you can push on them in your proposal.

So, let's take a look at a description:

✽ ✽ ✽

"We need assistance transitioning from our current marketplace (on Sharetribe) to a wordpress marketplace. See below information with a big emphasis on point number 3 and 4 as these are vital to our marketplace success. I have no problem manually moving over all the shops because I know that can't be automated, I just want everything ready to go before I get to that point.

3. Need a custom order page built into the theme similar to this (https://www.URLOBSCURED).

4. Need to integrate a closed messaging system that restricts outside communication on the platform."

❊ ❊ ❊

What do you think the key hiring criteria is?

The custom order page and messaging system, right? It's one of the things I always say... most clients will just come right out and tell you how to sell them.

What's NOT a key hiring criteria?

"Manually moving over the shops."

If you wrote a proposal where you failed to mention the custom order page and messaging system and focused mostly on how you could move over the shops, how do you think it'd perform?

It sounds kinda dumb to even think about.

Why would you do that?

Well, guess what happens when you copy/paste proposals or you don't take the time to read the project description in detail? If you don't mention something important they highlight in the description!

Good luck getting hired.

Now, this is a super clear example.

I wanted to use it so you could see it clearly. Sometimes, those criteria will be a little more subtle. Take this one, for example:

* * *

"Chicago Realtor looking for a digital marketing expert. Job entails:
Posting several times per week to social media (SEO, hashtags) and using analytics for best results

Post blog posts, add images

Knowledge in drip campaigns, Google Analytics- a plus"

* * *

Can you spot the big KHC?

Here's a hint...

If a client mentions something "is a plus", that's a big red flag signalling a way you can beat out the other people who might post on this job. If all else is equal, the client will go with the freelancer that *has* the "plus".

So, it's simple things like this.

One more big example. Upwork lets clients specify questions a freelancer must answer when they submit a proposal. Look at these carefully. You're not only going to have to answer them, but they are an indicator of something that's important to the client.

These are often KHCs, as well.

Okay, so go through your first project on the list and pull out any KHCs you find. Just make a note of them. We'll inject these into our proposal to add some "life" to it.

Which brings us finally to...

CHAPTER 15: WRITE YOUR PROPOSAL

NOW, we can write our proposal. We're in front of the right people on the right medium and we have an idea of what the right message is going to look like.

Now, here's the big secret to proposals:

CLIENTS DON'T CARE ABOUT YOU!

Sorry, they don't. They don't care how long you've been in this industry, where you went to school, how many projects you've successfully completed, what other clients say about you...

They don't REALLY care about any of that.

They care about themselves.

They care about what THEY want.

YOU are a means to an end.

I know... harsh. But true. But once you recognize this, writing your proposal becomes simple. It's NOT about you. It's about them. So, what can you do *for them*?

THAT is what they care about.

With that in mind...

The most effective way to get hired is to show a client examples of your work that match EXACTLY what they're after.

Simply do that and you'll land a good portion of your clients.

So, using our example from earlier, if I could show the clients examples of custom order pages and messaging systems I've created in the past, they'd probably trip over themselves trying to hire me.

Don't assume they'll see it in your portfolio.

No.

Put it in their face.

And this, again, goes all the way back to WHY picking your niche is so important. If you're bidding on random jobs, you likely WON'T have done anything like it before.

So, you won't have examples.

And, the client will hire the person that does.

If you do pick a niche, you'll have work examples of that exact thing BECAUSE you do the same thing on every project. You'll have tons of examples, in fact. Probably more than anyone else.

The client will think, "Whoa this is what he DOES."

See you as a specialist and hire you on the spot.

Even more, if you're brand new and don't have those work examples, it's worth spending some time getting them because you're not just going to stuff them in a portfolio.

They will be your MAIN sales tool.

From here, writing your proposal is straight-forward.

Here's an example:

"Hey, I'm John. I specialize in building custom order pages for e-commerce websites. You'll want to check the A, B and C projects in my portfolio to see examples of the exact kind of page you want.

As I said, this is what I do. I've built 35 of these custom order pages to date. I've built them for clients you might know like D, E and F. I've built them in industries like G, H and I.

Of course, I'm also well-versed in all the other aspects of building and running an e-commerce site and can help with whatever you need. In any case, take a look at my profile and portfolio and let me know if you'd like to proceed.

Thanks!

John"

Nothing super clever. Straight-forward, direct and clear. That said, there are a few key components:

- Intro. *Hi, I'm John...*
- Specialization Statement. *I specialize in...*
- Point to examples. *You'll want to check...*
- Proof. *Volume, name-drop and variety...*
- Cover the bases. *I'm also well-versed in...*
- Call to action. *Let me know if...*

These are the basic components of a quality proposal. Some of those you may not be able to include (based on your experience and/or the project) and that's fine. But the more of them you can integrate into your proposal, the better.

Now, you just need to press send. :)

Of course, there's a few other pieces here like answering the questions, pricing projects and so on (I cover those in my full course at: https://myjohn.us/r2), but when it comes to WRITING your proposal, these are the big pieces.

And, I've seen it time and time again.

The people who actually DO all this, in full faith, tend to get results and have success on Upwork. The people who struggle, just don't do it or try to shortcut it somehow.

There are no shortcuts.

Put in the work and you'll see the benefit.

So, there you go.

Okay, coming up, we're going to put all this on steroids. I'm going to show you a method to get eyeballs on your profile that most people think is crazy.

And, it IS counter-intuitive.

So much so, I think I'm the only person on the planet that teaches it.

But, once you SEE it...

Given everything you now know about Upwork...

It will make complete sense.

And, you'll chuckle at all the people dismissing it out of hand. The advantage it gives you on Upwork is untouchable. Anyway, that's for another day. Right now, get out there and get at least one proposal submitted using the method I just showed you.

And see what happens.

I think you might be surprised.

DAY 3: JUICE THE ALGORITHM

First, let's just take a step back. If you've made it this far and been implementing as we've gone along... you've already done a TON! So, give yourself a little pat on the back.

It's no small thing.

As I've said, most people just don't even do it. So, taking that action puts you miles ahead. Let's keep that rolling.

That said, are you ready to get a little crazy?

Actually, in my opinion, what we're about to do is the most sane, obvious thing you could do with Upwork. But, I do get called "crazy" from those who don't really understand Upwork.

And, why this work so well.

But, whatever... more for us, right?

So, what is this "crazy" new strategy?

Let me put it this way...

What if you could immediately eliminate any and all other competition on the projects you bid on? What if clients came

ready to hire you and ONLY you? And, you could "juice" Upwork's algorithm in your favor so you rapidly rise to the top of the Search and Suggestion Engine?

Sounds impossible I'm sure.

But, it's exactly what I did.

How?

CHAPTER 16: BYOC

Bring Your Own Clients. Said another way... run your Upwork business like every other business on the internet does. Don't rely on 100% on Upwork to bring you clients.

Beat feet and get some yourself.

Build an online audience...

And, have them hire you on Upwork.

STOP!

This is where the eyes usually start to roll and accusations of "crazy" start coming out.

"Why in the world would I GIVE Upwork my clients?"

First, if you're Top Rated or Rising Talent on Upwork, you can bring your client over and pay 0% fees. So, you're literally losing nothing to do it. But, even if you have to pay the fees, it's still worth it, IMO.

Why?

Because, job history is GOLD on Upwork.

The more and better job history you have, the more you're going to get suggested to future clients and the more of those jobs you'll land.

Let me ask you...

What do you think happens when the largest freelancing platform on the planet, that has thousands of new jobs posted every single day, suddenly sees YOU as a top freelancer in your niche?

I'll tell you.

More job invites than you could ever possibly accept.

Jobs literally being thrown at you.

And, in the long-run, you'll obviously earn more.

I also happen to know a few top-earning freelancers on Upwork, guys who've earned 200K, 300K and up on the platform and this is their "dirty little secret".

They grind on Upwork itself, for sure.

But, they bring all their clients there, as well.

And, that just continually juices the algorithm in their favor.

So, the basic idea is you bring your own clients to Upwork in order to build your job history. That job history then gets you more attention on Upwork which gets you clients you might not otherwise have got. That builds your job history even more... and the cycle repeats.

If every project you brought to Upwork netted you even just one more you wouldn't have gotten otherwise, isn't that worth it? Even IF you're paying the Upwork fee for the clients you bring.

I'll answer because I've done it: It *is* worth it.

That said, I'm not going to beat you over the head with this. I know it's not for everybody. But, if you're up for getting a little "crazy", this is a big competitive advantage you can create for yourself.

So, with that said, let's dig into the HOW...

CHAPTER 17: PICK A PLATFORM

I recommend you pick a platform to begin with... as in singular. It's easy to get spread too thin and spend too much time on platforms that aren't bringing you any results. You only need a strong following on one of the major platforms to get a lot of traction with this.

But, you also shouldn't pick just *any* platform.

You should pick the ones that fit best with your business.

Here's a basic breakdown:

- Instagram: Graphic designers, artists, etc.
- YouTube: Developers
- Medium: Writers
- Twitter/LinkedIn: Copywriters, sales business, etc.

That's not the end-all, be-all list, but it does generally tend to hold true. Those platforms are simply tailored to those categories. But, you will find good developer communities on Instagram, for example.

Go with what fits YOU and your services best. You want to reduce friction as much as possible.

CHAPTER 18: BUILD A PROFILE PATHWAY

The whole point here is to get people to hire you on Upwork. So, you need to point them there. On platforms like Twitter and Instagram, profiles are prominent. So, you want to make sure and write a profile bio that pushes your followers to hiring you.

On other platforms like YouTube, profiles are less prominent. So, we'll do that pushing more in our content. Which we'll get to in a minute. That said, here's a basic formula for writing your profile bio:

- Specialty
- Proof
- Call to Action

Look familiar? Very similar to what we're doing on our Upwork profile, we just have less words we can use. Here's an example:

"I'm a freelance graphic designer that specializes in creating logos for small businesses. I graduated from the Rhode Island School of Design and have been a designer for 10+ years. You can learn more about hiring me for your project on Upwork here: URL"

You'll have to tighten that up depending on the platform you're on, but that's the basic idea. It's simple, but it opens the door and lets people know 1) what you do and 2) you're available for hire.

People WILL click through.

CHAPTER 19: FISHERMAN FORMULA

When a pro fishes, he doesn't just toss out his hook and hope for the best. Quite the opposite, in fact. Professional fishermen geek out on the "science" of fishing. They could talk about it for hours.

What bait to use and why, where to fish, what time of day, time of year. That's HOW they catch fish so easily. Social media *is* fishing... for clients and customers. And, the science is just as important.

In particular, the BAIT.

So, what we need to do now is post content that will simultaneously attract and soft-sell our ideal clients. This is why the right platform is so important. Posting the right kind of content *for the platform* is like tossing fresh meat into a pool of piranhas. They'll swarm.

If you're a graphic designer, Instagram is MADE for you. Post pictures of your designs. If they're good, you'll build a following.

If you're a writer, Twitter is your friend. Post your long-form content on Medium or your own blog. But, you can take little bits of what you write and turn it into 10, 15 or more tweets. In fact, I will take what I'm writing to you right now and turn it into 2 or 3 days worth of tweets. Not long threads. Just small, disjointed tweets. People love that stuff on there. It really is that simple.

If you're a developer, post tutorials on YouTube. Brad Traversy, a famous YouTube developer, has 1.21 million subscribers to his YouTube channel and that's all he does.

The right bait on the right platform.

I can't stress that enough.

But, where do you get ideas for content?

Gary Vaynerchuk has the best advice when it comes to this: "Document don't create." Don't try to think of things to create. Just document what you're already doing.

If you don't have client work, just make stuff. If you're a developer, build some websites or apps just for practice or fun. If you're a graphic designer, design some graphics. Writers... write. And, so on.

This is your life's work. It's what you love doing and, if you're new, you need the practice anyway. So, create! That's what creators don.

And then, post what you make on social media. Document your process. Share things you learn. Etc. Once you embrace that mindset, you'll have access to more content than you could ever just "think up".

At the end of the day, we just want to make sure we're constantly posting new content to our platform AND ensure that content is the kind that will attract people who want to hire us. Again... *relevance.*

CHAPTER 20: GET SOCIAL

This is the piece most business people miss. They focus on what THEY are posting and forget that social media is... well... social. It's about building relationships.

What's the #1 thing EVERYBODY on social media wants?

Attention.

They don't want to comment on YOUR stuff; they want YOU to comment on THEIR stuff. Just think how quickly you flip open your social media when you get notified of a new comment.

So, use that to your advantage.

Spend most of your time on social commenting on other people's stuff. Just make sure that the posts you comment on are from people whose AUDIENCE are your ideal clients.

So, find other influencers in your niche.

Follow them.

And, post on their stuff everyday.

Our man, Gary Vee, recommends 90-100 comments per day. It's a lot. But, even if you only make 50… that's better than 20 or 10 or 1. So, as much as you can. Comment, comment comment.

And, I'm just telling you.

It works.

I did about 40-50 a day for a month on Instagram and tripled my following in that time. That was after years of NOT doing it and getting almost no followers.

When you comment on other people's social media posts, they and they people who follow them will see it and become interested in who you are. So, they click through to your profile which is full of cool, relevant content and is optimized for sending people to your Upwork profile.

And, it just plain works.

Said another way… If you comment, they will come.

CHAPTER 21: PROMOTE

Now, we need to directly promote your services on Upwork. There's two ways to include promotions in your posts:

- Small snippet in every post
- One big ad every 5-10 posts

Which one you choose comes down to what you're most comfortable with AND your audience. Pick one and test. For the "small snippet" approach, check the end of this chapter for an example.

With the "one big ad" approach, the big key is to have a compelling reason each time. So, don't just post a "buy my stuff" ad. You want to create urgency by offering something time-limited.

A discount.

A bonus.

Or, "I'm only taking X new clients".

Something that gives them a compelling reason to act NOW. All the work you do in your other posts to build authority and create goodwill will pay off IF you create a bit of urgency.

Otherwise, it will tend to fall flat.

And, just keep it that simple. Post regularly. Document don't create. Comment, comment, comment... then, comment some more. And, occasionally, sell your stuff.

Your following will grow.

And, it only takes a client or two, every once in awhile dropped in over on Upwork to juice the algorithm in your favor. Before you know it, you'll be rolling and nothing can stop you!

As I mentioned, I think I'm the only person in the world who teaches this (Though, I know I'm NOT the only one who DOES it), but it's the most foolproof way to win on Upwork.

You almost can't lose.

That's why I spend just short of 2 hours walking you line-by-line through this in my full Upwork course. I break down the major social media platforms and how to run this strategy on each.

Plus blogging, email and podcasting.

I do a full breakdown of exactly how I write my daily content that inspires, entertains, educates and sells. If you see the power of this strategy, this course is the ultimate training on it.

You can learn more about the course here: **https://myjohn.us/r2**

CHAPTER 22: TLDR

Let's take a minute and recap everything we've covered in this book, so far. Here's a run-down of the basic ideas I've outlined:

As a new Upworker, you're at a disadvantage because you don't have an extensive job history and reviews like established Upworkers.

The way around that is to give clients a compelling reason to pick you over those other more experienced Upworkers. In this case, that reason is specialization. You do exactly what they need and it's all you do.

This strategy not only makes clients more likely to hire you, but also ensures that Upwork only shows your profile (in Search and Suggestion listings) to clients looking for the exact service you offer, thus increasing the likelihood that you get hired.

As your job history grows on Upwork, you can expand to larger, higher traffic keywords and get even more work.

Ergo... everything we do, from how we build our profiles to what jobs we bid, etc is oriented around this strategy.

And, if you really want to go all-in on Upwork, start getting clients outside the platform (content marketing, social media, networking, etc) and bring them to Upwork in order to build your job history on the site and bring you even more clients down the road.

That's the basic gist of it. Of course, details matter... how you build your profile, what you say in your overview, what you include in your portfolio, what jobs you bid on, what you put in your proposals, how you deliver, and so on.

The aim of this book was to give you the basics to get you started (because those basic are a lot on their own). And, if you're ready for the advanced training to get even more clients from Upwork, you can check out my full 6-hour course at: **https://myjohn.us/r2**.

I hope you enjoyed the book. If you did, I'd really appreciate a positive review on Amazon. You can also jump on my free freelance tips newsletter at **https://johnmorrisonline.com**.

APPENDIX A: THE PSYCHOLOGY OF HIGH-PAYING CLIENTS

One of the fundamental principles I teach in my general freelancing courses goes as follows: Charge more, make more, work less.

This isn't a list of goals. It's a process and a way of thinking about HOW to build your freelance business that catapults you from being overworked, underpaid and underappreciated to appreciated and well paid with tons of free time for the things and people you love.

Charging more shouldn't be some thing you "hope" to do. It's a necessity. If you "start low and stay low", you will eventually get burnt out and likely give up. I've seen it happen time and time again.

But, as the saying goes:

"You can't squeeze blood out of turnip."

You can't get something from people that they don't have. That means in order to charge more, you have to find clients who are willing and able to pay more. I know, rocket surgery.

But, a lot of freelancers get lost when thinking about all this; trying to get clients, who CANnot or WILL not pay more, to accept higher prices. You'll be much better off finding the people who are already there.

To do that, you have to understand how they think. Unlike the clients you're used to, their primary concern is NOT price. It's actually not even quality like so many people assume.

If I had to give it a word, I'd go with:

Brainpower.

Premium clients don't want to have to expend their brainpower on the projects they hire you for. They don't want to have to provide constant direction and motivation.

They want YOU to do that.

They want to be able to hand a project off to you and TRUST that you'll not only get it done, but get it done right. With "right" being what you, as the expert, know to be right and can explain to them; NOT them telling you what right looks like.

They can do that with anybody. They want somebody they don't HAVE to do that with. Often times, they're successful people who are busy and have a lot on their plate.

What they want more than anything is the "mental" weight of the project off their shoulders so they can focus on other things. They're also used to being let down so they tend to be jaded and skeptical.

With all that said, your service AND delivery must have a few key qualities to attract these kinds of clients, make them happy and keep them hiring you. And yes, it's worth it. Just one or two of these kinds of clients could be all you need to run a six-figure business.

What are those key qualities?

Let's jump into them...

CHAPTER 23: TURNKEY

Google defines turnkey as: "a complete product or service that is ready for immediate use". That sums it up quite well. High-paying clients want solutions that are comprehensive and ready to just plug in immediately.

If they're hiring someone to run their Google advertising, for example, they don't want someone to *tell them* what to do or to provide "suggestions". No. They want YOU to do it and it *all*.

"Just take it off my plate so I don't have to think about it."

Your solution should require as little input from the client as possible. Sure, you'll always need *some*, but that should come at the beginning and shouldn't require more than a meeting or two.

After that, you take over and run things. You tell them what needs done and then *you* do it. Clients will pay for this. Clients with money are *dying* for this and, if you deliver, they'll never let you go.

CHAPTER 24: RESULTS-ORIENTED.

You'll be hard-pressed to charge $10,000 for a logo. I imagine there's somebody out there that can and does, but it's not likely. More than that, though, you'll have a tough time landing high-paying clients if you offer vague or intangible results.

A celebrity, for example, is less likely to pay through the nose for "general fitness advice", but likely would pay top dollar to "get ripped abs to land the movie role I really want".

Many often do.

Same with businesspeople. They're not likely to pay top dollar for an "e-commerce expert", but will pay a premium for a marketer who can "increase ROI by 300%".

You need to show you can get results.

And, to be frank, some services aren't great fits for this kind of approach. Using our logo design example, it's going to be tough to connect your designs to increased ROI or sales.

The trick is add-on services that DO easily connect.

If you build websites, add SEO or SEM to your offering. If you're a graphic designer, add UI/UX to your offering. If you're a writer, add copywriting to your offering.

The more you can make a client feel like they're trading dollars for dollars (pay me $1,000 and I'll make you $10,000), the more they're going to be willing to pay for your services.

CHAPTER 25: FLAWLESS

If you paid somebody $10,000 for... anything, what would your expectations be? Would you expect to have to hunt them down for updates? Would you expect them to be late to meetings?

Would you expect anything less than perfection?

You wouldn't. High-paying clients are the same. They expect perfection. Now, nobody is perfect. I get it. But, that's what you have to strive for. So, that the few, small mistakes that do inevitably pop up don't snowball into an avalanche of disappointment.

My best piece of advice here?

Systems and science. As much as you can, turn everything into a process or system. Write it down, scope it out... refine, refine, refine until you get as close to perfect as you possibly can.

Then, refine some more.

Eventually, you'll reach a point where YOU are the only one who notices when something goes wrong. That's freelancing Nirvana.

ABOUT THE AUTHOR

John Morris

John Morris is a former salesman, military instructor, developer, and copywriter with over 20 years of experience in the digital marketing world. As an online entrepreneur, John has created over 30 online courses that have attracted over 40,000 students and has garnered millions of views on YouTube. He has sold millions of  dollars in products and services both online and off, making him a respected authority in the world of marketing.

When he's not working, John enjoys spending time with his wife and four kids, cheering on his favorite football team, the Huskers, and hitting the gym to pursue his passion for bodybuilding. With a love for all things superheroes, John's enthusiasm for life is infectious, and his book is sure to inspire readers to reach new heights in their freelance careers.

You can join his free newsletter where he regularly shares tips on freelancing, influence, marketing, persuasion, and more at: https://johnmorrisonline.com.

PRAISE FOR AUTHOR

"John is the man! I followed his steps and I am flooded with interviews in a week. I got into two Talent clouds. The very next day, I got an invitation from the talent specialists from Upwork and a lot more. I wanna shout out, he is the best in this. Thanks John for helping me out!"

--Jithin Veedu

"After viewing John's course, I made an Upwork account and it got approved the same day. Amazingly, I got my first job the very same day, I couldn't believe it, I thought maybe I got it by coincidence. Anyways I completed the job and received my first earnings. Then, after two days, I got another job and within a week I got 3 jobs and completed them successfully. All the things he says seem to be minute but have a very great impact on your freelancing career."

--Divyendra Singh Jadoun

"I started this 3 days ago, following John's suggestions, and I gained the Upwork Rising Talent badge in less than 2 days. I have a call with my first potential client tomorrow. Thanks, John!"

--Stephanie Korski

"I have been following John Morris for several years now. His instruction ranges from beginner to advanced, to CEO-level guidance. I have referred friends and clients to John, and have encouraged my own daughter to pay attention to what he says. All of his teachings create wealth for me (and happiness for my clients!) I can't speak highly enough about John, his name is well known in my home."

--Scott Plude

"I've been in an existential crisis for the last week about what the heck I'm doing as a business owner. Even though I've been a business for about a year, I'm constantly trying to think of how to prune and refine services. This was very personable and enjoyable to watch. Usually, business courses like this are dry and hard to get through…. repeating the same things over and over again. This was a breath of fresh air. THANK YOU."

--Sarah Mui

"I've definitely learnt so much in 2.5 hours than I'd learn watching different videos online on Youtube and reading tons of articles on the web. John has a natural way of teaching, where he is passionately diving in the topics and he makes it very easy to grasp — someone who wants you to really start running your business well by learning about the right tools and implement them in your online business. I will definitely share with many of the people I know who have been struggling for so long, I did find my answers and I'm sure will do too."

--Waqas Abdul Majeed

"By the way, just hit 95K for the year. I can't thank you enough for everything you've taught me. You've changed my life. Thank you!"

--Michael Phoenix

"75 SEO and website clients now. My income went from sub zero to over 6K just last month. Tracking 10K for next month. Seriously, you changed my life."

--Tim Covello

"John has been the most important person in my freelance career ever since I started. Without him, I would have taken 10 or 20 years more to reach the position I am at now (Level 2 seller on Fiverr and Top Rated on Upwork)."

--Misrab Mohamed

"John is a fantastic and patient tutor, who is not just able to share knowledge and communicate it very effectively – but able to support one in applying it. However, I believe that John has a very rare ability to go further than just imparting knowledge and showing one how to apply it. He is able to innately provoke one's curiosity when explaining and demonstrating concepts, to the extent that one can explore and unravel their own learning journey. Thanks very much John!"

--Sukh Plaha

"John has provided expert knowledge and advice on multiple occasions that have helped me better serve my clients. John is a Rockstar!"

--Steve Dimmick

"John Morris is exceptional in his ability to give focused insight into Freelancing and starting one's business. His direct methods inspire confidence in his honesty."

--Andrew Malone

"I recommend John every chance I get. If every person I worked with were as committed to excellence, punctuality, value, and unquestionable integrity… the world would be a better place. Highest recommendation."

--Ray Edwards

"John is amazing!"

--Lewis Howes

www.ingramcontent.com/pod-product-compliance
Lightning Source LLC
Chambersburg PA
CBHW050249220526
45465CB00002B/616